Pre-mix...

There is a growing consu

food bills by preparing r

nutritious food.

A poll of men and women across a range of age groups conducted on Facebook in August 2008 found their main issue with cookery books in the UK is that the ingredients used are too expensive. Nearly half the women polled believe this to be the case. Over a third of the men polled said that they find cookery books too daunting and off putting.

In recent years there have been very few 'back to basics' cookery books available – until now.

mix. is a comprehensive guide to basic proportions in cookery, giving the quantities needed for simple, everyday family food. Containing over 170 recipes, from how to make a white sauce to how to prepare pastry, this is an essential cookery book for young people who want to learn to cook, families interested in saving money on food bills and teachers and students of Home Economics/Food Technology.

"A fantastic concise book explaining everyday recipes and giving every cook a helping hand with the secret of successful cookery... getting the basics right first!"

Antony Worrall Thompson

Contents

savoury.

mix.

aiöli. batter. béarnaise
sauce. bolognaise
sauce. tomato sauce.
casserole. fish cakes.
couscous. gravy. mint
sauce. hollandaise sauce.
poached fish. omelette.
pesto. quiche. rice.
risotto. savoury shortcrust
pastry. savoury roulade.
savoury soufflé. shepherd's
pie. soup. stuffing.
vinaigrette. white sauce.

aïöli.

Serve in fish soup, over fish, or with crisp blanched vegetables or French fries.

makes enough for **4**

3 egg yolks
4 garlic cloves
Juice of ½ lemon
Salt and freshly ground black pepper
150ml extra virgin olive oil

Here's how to make it...

- Blend all of the ingredients together in a blender except the oil.
- Add the oil in a steady stream until it forms a thick sauce.

Variations

Orange aïöli *Grated zest of 1 orange and juice of ½ orange. Add instead of lemon juice.*

Saffron aïöli *1 pinch of saffron blended with 2 tsp boiling water, cooled before adding.*

Mustard aïöli *Add ½ tsp English mustard powder or 1 tsp wholegrain mustard.*

James says...

For a funky serving approach when feeding lots of people, add 3 tbsp cold water and serve in a small teapot.

batter.

In essence two basic types of batter exist: coating and pouring. Used for pancakes, dropped scones, toad-in-the hole, Yorkshire puddings or fritters etc, batter is quick and versatile.

	Plain flour	Salt	Liquid	Egg
Thin batter: Toad-in-the-hole, Yorkshire puddings, Pancakes, Dropped scones	100g	Pinch	275ml milk	1
Coating batter: Deep fried fish or poultry	100g	Pinch	150ml milk	1
Fritter batter: Banana, apple or pineapple fritters, Courgette or squash fritters, Sausage fritters	50g	Pinch	3 tbsp water 3 tbsp vegetable oil	1 egg white

Here's how to make it...

- Sieve flour and salt into a bowl. Make a well in the centre.
- Put the egg and half of the liquid into the well. Using a balloon whisk, gently whisk to a smooth batter. Add the rest of the liquid and beat for a few moments.
- Alternatively, place all of the ingredients into a blender and whizz until combined.

James says...

If food is to be coated in batter, it must be dry, so dab with kitchen paper before coating.

béarnaise sauce.

A classic sauce to serve with steak.

makes enough for 4

1 tbsp fresh chopped tarragon or 1½ tsp dried
2½ tbsp vinegar
Salt and freshly ground black pepper
2 egg yolks
1 tbsp cold water
125g butter, cut into 1 cm cubes
Juice of ½ lemon

Here's how to make it...

- Place tarragon, vinegar and seasoning into a pan and reduce by two thirds. Allow to cool slightly.
- In a small bowl, beat yolks and water together and add to the pan with vinegar. Heat gently, whisking vigorously until it starts to thicken.
- Add butter, a cube at a time, whisking vigorously until combined.
- Whisk in lemon juice.
- Serve.

James says...

If serving with a steak, ensure you oil and season the steak not the pan. Use a cast iron grill pan and get it really hot before adding the steak. Cook for 3 minutes on one side and 3 on the other. Remove from pan, place onto a cold plate and allow to rest for 10 minutes before eating.

bolognaise sauce.

Easy to make, versatile and arguably the nation's favourite dish.

1 tbsp vegetable oil
1 small onion, chopped
1 small stick celery, chopped
50g mushrooms, sliced
25g plain flour
1 x 400g can chopped tomatoes
125ml stock
1 tbsp Worcestershire sauce
Salt and freshly ground black pepper
250g minced beef
2 tbsp freshly chopped basil

Here's how to make it...

- Heat the oil in a saucepan and gently fry the vegetables for about 5 minutes until soft but not coloured. Stir in the flour.
- Add the tomatoes, stock, sauce, seasoning and mince, cover and simmer for 45 minutes.
- Stir in basil.
- Serve with freshly boiled spaghetti.

James says...

If a vegetarian Bolognaise is required, add 500g of mixed chopped vegetables including pepper, aubergine and courgette instead of mince and simmer for 25 minutes.

tomato sauce.

A versatile sauce for pasta.

serves 4

1 tbsp vegetable oil
1 small onion, chopped
1 clove garlic, crushed
1 x 400g can chopped tomatoes
½ tsp sugar
Salt and freshly ground black pepper
Pinch grated nutmeg
1 tbsp lemon juice mixed with 1 tbsp cornflour
2 tbsp freshly chopped basil

Here's how to make it...

- Heat the oil in a saucepan and gently sauté the onion and garlic for 5 minutes.
- Add all other ingredients except the basil and bring to the boil. Reduce the heat and simmer for 2 minutes.
- Add basil and serve.

James says...

It's important to add the fresh chopped basil at the end so it remains fresh in flavour and aromatic.

casserole.

I love a good casserole served with mashed potatoes. Well, coming from Northern Ireland, really I love anything with potatoes!

2 tbsp plain flour
Salt and freshly ground black pepper
900g meat, diced
2 tbsp vegetable oil
1 onion, chopped
500g root vegetables, peeled and chopped
300ml stock

Here's how to make it...

- Mix the flour with the seasoning and toss the meat in it.
- Heat the vegetable oil in a large casserole and fry off the meat in 3 batches to brown. Remove and set aside.
- Sauté the onion in the casserole for 2–3 minutes until soft and then replace the meat.
- Add the vegetables and stock and bring to the boil. Place the lid on top.
- Place into a preheated oven at 180°C (160°C if using a fan oven) or Gas Mark 4 for at least 2 hours.
- **2, 3 and 4 Oven Aga,** cook in the Simmering Oven for at least 2 hours.
- **Rayburn,** cook on the 4th set of runners in the Main Oven with the Thermodial reading Simmer for at least 2 hours.

James says...

It's important to add the flour to the meat as this thickens the casserole while it cooks.

fish cakes.

A really quick dinner or lunch using leftovers, or canned fish.

makes

250g cooked or canned fish
250g cooked and mashed potato
Salt and freshly ground black pepper
1 tsp lemon juice
1 egg, beaten
Fresh bread crumbs
1 egg, beaten

Here's how to make it...

- Remove the bones and skin from cooked fish. Flake and mash onto a plate.
- Add fish to mashed potato, beat until smooth.
- Season and add lemon juice and egg. Beat together.
- Form mixture into a large roll on a floured surface, cut into 10 rounds and dip in egg and breadcrumbs.
- Fry in a hot frying pan with a little oil on both sides until browned.
- Serve.

Variations

Spicy fish cakes *Add ½ chopped red chilli to mix.*

James says...

Fresh breadcrumbs are easy to make by popping some stale bread into a food processor and whizzing.

couscous.

An easy, no-cook alternative to potatoes, rice, pasta and other carbs.

225g couscous
1 bunch fresh parsley, chopped
1 bunch fresh coriander, chopped
1 red onion, chopped
Zest and juice of 1 lemon
2 tbsp sunflower seeds, toasted
2 tbsp sesame seeds, toasted
4 tbsp extra virgin olive oil
Salt and freshly ground black pepper

Here's how to make it...

- Place the couscous in a bowl with twice its volume of hot water or stock and leave to soak for 10 minutes.
- Mix all the remaining ingredients together and stir through. Leave for 30 minutes to allow flavours to develop.

Variations

Apricot, almond and chickpea couscous *Leave out the seeds but add 2 tbsp toasted flaked almonds, 1 can chickpeas, drained and 200g chopped ready-to-eat dried apricots.*

Mint and lemon couscous *Add 1 bunch freshly chopped mint and the grated zest of 2 lemons.*

Mushroom couscous *Leave out the seeds and add 100g chopped and sautéed mushrooms.*

Spicy couscous *Using the recipe above or any of the variations, why not add some harissa marinade or harissa paste? It's a very spicy Moroccan paste that's added to tajines and other Moroccan food. Remember with harissa, less is more.*

James says...

Couscous is a small granular type of pasta from North Africa, most famously Morocco. Flavoured couscous can be bought in supermarkets, but I find it tastes a lot better when you flavour your own.

gravy.

It's an essential part of a Sunday roast.

Juices and sediment from roast
1 tbsp plain flour
Crushed stockcube
Glass red wine or white wine for poultry
Vegetable water

Here's how to make it...

- Remove excess fat from roasting tin and stir flour through using a balloon whisk. Add stock cube and wine and place on top of hob to reduce.
- Thin down with vegetable water.
- **2, 3 and 4 Oven Aga,** after adding flour, stock and wine, place onto floor of the Roasting Oven for 3–4 minutes and thin with vegetable water.
- **Rayburn,** after adding flour, stock and wine, place onto floor of the Main Oven for 3–4 minutes after cooking roast and thin with vegetable water.

James says...

Make as thick or thin as you require by adding more or less flour.

mint sauce.

Delicious with roast lamb.

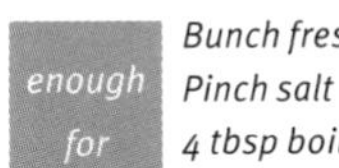

Bunch fresh mint
Pinch salt
4 tbsp boiling water
4 tbsp white wine vinegar
1 tbsp caster sugar

Here's how to make it...

- Strip the mint leaves off the stalks, sprinkle with salt and chop finely.
- Place into a jug, add the sugar and pour over boiling water. Stir and leave to cool.
- Stir in vinegar, serve or refrigerate.

James says...

So you don't miss out during the winter months, why not make this when mint is in season and freeze?

hollandaise sauce.

Takes a little bit of effort, but it's well worth it. Serve warm over fish or freshly cooked asparagus.

makes enough to serve **4**

3 tbsp white wine vinegar
6 peppercorns
4 egg yolks
250g butter
Juice ½ lemon
Salt and freshly ground black pepper

Here's how to make it...

- Put the vinegar in a small pan with the peppercorns, bring to the boil and reduce by half. Remove the peppercorns and discard.
- Place the egg yolks into a blender or food processor with the vinegar.
- Gently melt the butter so that the butter solids fall to the bottom of the pan.
- Turn on the blender and slowly pour the butter in with the motor running. The sauce will start to thicken. Don't pour the butter solids in that are at the bottom of the pan.
- Add lemon juice and seasoning.

James says...

Traditionally a hollandaise was made in a bain marie over a pan of simmering water and whisked by hand. The blender approach is a lot quicker.

poached fish.

Very easy to do. As the fish is being cooked in liquid the smell won't permeate the kitchen.

serves as many as you like

Poaching liquid, eg milk, cider or stock, enough to half cover fish
Fish steaks or fillets
1 bay leaf
6 peppercorns

Here's how to make it...

- Place the fish in a pan, cover with the liquid and add the bay leaf and peppercorns.
- Heat gently, not allowing it to boil.
- Simmer for time in table below.

Fish	Time to poach
175–200g fillets	*6–8 minutes*
Whole trout	*8–10 minutes*
Salmon steaks	*6–8 minutes*

James says...

Why not use the poaching liquid to make a sauce? See page 48 for how to make a roux.

omelette.

Great for a quick lunch or for using leftovers.

3 eggs
Salt and freshly ground black pepper
15g butter
25g grated cheese
50–100g chopped and sautéed mushrooms

Here's how to make it...

- Prove an omelette pan by sprinkling with salt and heating gently. Clean out with a paper towel. Heat a small piece of butter in the pan, allow to darken in colour, discard. The pan is now ready to use.
- Beat the eggs well until increased in volume and season.
- Melt the butter until it sizzles, pour in the egg slowly. Using a spatula or fish slice, drag some of the omelette mix towards you, and then pour some of the uncooked mix into the space. Keep doing this until all of the egg mix is cooked.
- Place some of the filling onto the nearside half of the omelette, fold the other side over and serve warm.

Variations

Chicken and tomato *Use about 50g cooked chicken per person and 1 chopped tomato.*

Ham and cheese *Chop 1 to 2 slices of ham per person (depending on size) and use as filling with grated cheese.*

Bacon and cheese *Sauté 1–2 slices of chopped bacon per person, mix with the grated cheese.*

James says...

Don't overcook an omelette or it will go tough. I find it best to call everyone to the table before starting to make an omelette.

pesto.

Pesto made at home is full of fresh flavours and a lot nicer than the stuff in jars from the supermarkets. It's a cold, no-cook sauce that can be added to pasta dishes and has a thick pouring consistency.

25g pine nuts
Leaves of 1 large basil plant, washed
2 garlic cloves, peeled
1 tsp sea salt
50g freshly grated Parmesan or Pecorino cheese
200ml extra virgin olive oil

Here's how to make it...

- Heat a saucepan and toast the pine nuts gently for 1–2 minutes.
- Place all the items into a blender or food processor and whizz until it looks like a green sauce.
- Serve with freshly cooked pasta, bread or boiled new potatoes.

Variations

Watercress and walnut pesto *Replace the basil with a large bunch of watercress and add 25g of walnut pieces instead of pine nuts. Walnuts don't toast as well as pine nuts, so just pop them in raw.*

Parsley pesto *Wash a large bunch of curly leaf parsley and swap for the basil.*

Coriander and chilli pesto *Wash a large bunch of coriander and remove the stalks. Add ½–1 red or green chilli. (Keep the seeds in for extra heat.) Whizz together as above.*

Rocket and brazil nut pesto *Use a large bunch of rocket instead of the basil. Replace the pine nuts with brazil nuts.*

James says...

Although pesto will keep in the fridge, or even freeze, it's at its best when eaten fresh. Why not grow some herbs at home?

quiche.

Great for lunches, picnics or even starters. Quiche is filling and a brilliant way of using leftovers.

Lines a pie dish or **4 smaller individual** *ones*

1 quantity savoury shortcrust pastry (see recipe 18, page 34)
Filling - see variations opposite
2 eggs
150ml double cream

Here's how to make it...

- If using an electric or gas oven, ensure the pastry is baked before cooking. If using an Aga or Rayburn, there is no need to bake the pastry before assembling the quiche, providing a flat-based quiche dish is used.
- Place quiche filling into the pastry (see opposite).
- Mix together eggs and cream with a fork until no more egg can be seen and add to quiche.
- Place into a preheated oven at 180°C (160°C if using a fan oven) or Gas Mark 4 for 30 minutes or until set.
- **2, 3 and 4 Oven Aga,** cook on the floor of the Roasting Oven for 30 minutes.
- **Rayburn,** cook on the floor of the Main Oven with the Thermodial reading Roast for 30 minutes.

Variations

Roast Mediterranean vegetable *Roughly chop up 1 aubergine, 1 courgette and 3 different coloured peppers. Place on a baking tray with 1 x 250g punnet cherry tomatoes. Mix with 2 tbsp oil and 3 tbsp balsamic vinegar, roast at 250°C or Gas Mark 8 for 20 minutes, or on the floor of the Aga Roasting Oven or the floor of the Rayburn with Thermodial reading Roast for 20 minutes. Place vegetables into pastry and crumble 1 packet of feta cheese on top. Add egg and cream mixture.*

Leek and apple *Chop 2 leeks and 1 onion, sweat in a pan until soft. Place into pastry case and add 1 Bramley apple that has been chopped up and 1 tbsp Calvados (optional). Sprinkle over some chopped St Agur cheese. Add eggs and cream.*

James says...

A quiche is ready when it's lightly coloured on top, the filling is set and the pastry is crisp. The liquid quantities in this recipe look small, but will be more than enough. If you don't want to use double cream, you can use 150ml milk and 3 eggs.

rice.

A 20-minute, no-fuss cook that can be served plain on the side or as a dish.

50g *makes* **1** *serving*

Allow 50g rice and 100ml water or stock per person
Pinch of salt

Here's how to make it...

- Place rice, water and salt into a pan and bring to the boil. If using a cast iron pan, place the lid on, remove from the heat and leave for 20 minutes – it's important to keep the lid on. If using any other type of pan, bring to the boil, reduce to a simmer, keep the lid on and leave for 20 minutes.
- **2, 3 and 4 Oven Aga,** bring to the boil, place the lid on top and place into the Simmering Oven for 20 minutes.
- **Rayburn,** bring to the boil, place the lid on top and place into the Lower Oven for 20 minutes with the Thermodial reading between Bake and Roast.

Variations

Salmon rice *Sauté an onion in the pan you're making the rice in. Add the rice and cook gently for a few moments before adding 100ml vegetable or chicken stock for every 50g rice. Cook as above and add some tinned or freshly cooked and flaked salmon. Stir through.*

Chicken rice *Sauté an onion in the pan you're making the rice in. Add the rice and cook gently for a few moments before adding 100ml vegetable or chicken stock for every 50g rice. Cook as above and then stir in some cooked chicken.*

Vegetable rice *Sauté an onion in the pan you're making the rice in. Add the rice and cook gently for a few moments before adding 100ml vegetable stock for every 50g rice. Cook as above and then add some roasted or blanched vegetables.*

James says...

Any of the absorption methods described above, either using the Aga or Rayburn, or indeed a cast iron casserole that retains its heat, will give you perfectly fluffy rice that has absorbed all the water and has not stuck together.

risotto.

This recipe needs a little bit of attention while cooking, but the results are worth it.

serves **4**

25g butter
1 small onion, chopped
250g risotto rice
500ml stock
Salt and freshly ground black pepper
3 tbsp Parmesan cheese, grated.
Filling - choose from variations opposite

Here's how to make it...

- Using a heavy-based pan, melt the butter and soften the onion until tender.
- Add rice and fry for about 2 minutes.
- Add one third of the stock, bring to the boil and cook for 20 minutes until the rice is tender, adding the remaining stock gradually as required. Stir as little as possible.
- Season and add fillings. Stir through Parmesan.

Variations

Mushroom *Add 100g chopped and sautéed mushrooms.*

Asparagus and bacon *Add 100g chopped and blanched asparagus tips and 3 slices of chopped fried bacon.*

Pea and mint *Add 100g frozen peas and 1 small bunch chopped mint.*

Chicken *Add 150g cooked chicken, chopped.*

James says...

It's important to add the stock a bit at a time and not to stir too much so as to prevent the rice from oozing too much starch.

savoury shortcrust pastry.

A useful recipe for all sorts of savoury products, either as a base or a lid.

Lines a **23cm** *pie dish or* **4 smaller individual** *ones*

200g plain flour, sieved
½ level tsp salt
100g butter or margarine, cut into small cubes, chilled
3 tbsp cold water

Here's how to make it...

- Place the flour and salt into a bowl. Add the fat and rub in. To rub in, take a little of the flour and some butter in your hands and press it between your thumb and small finger, moving your thumb up through all of your fingers. Repeat until mixture looks like fine breadcrumbs. Alternatively, place fat and flour into a food processor and blitz for a few seconds.
- Add water and mix together using a table knife. Knead lightly and place into the fridge to rest for 20 minutes before rolling out.
- If baking blind to make a pastry case, bake at 200°C (180°C if using a fan oven) or Gas Mark 7. Place some greaseproof paper over the pastry and fill with baking beans or rice before cooking. After 15 minutes, remove paper to colour the pastry. There's no need to bake blind if using an Aga or Rayburn, providing the pastry is in a flat bottomed dish on the floor of the Aga Roasting Oven or the floor of the Rayburn Main Oven with the Thermodial reading Roast. Just add the liquid filling to the raw pastry base before cooking.

Variations

Cheese *Add 50g mature Cheddar cheese and 1 tsp English mustard powder to the pastry after rubbing in the fat and flour.*

Poppyseed *Add 1 tbsp poppyseeds to the pastry after rubbing in the fat and flour.*

Herb *Add 1 tbsp freshly chopped herbs to the pastry after rubbing in the fat and flour.*

James says...

Pastry is commonly available in all supermarkets, but it is cheaper to make your own. My 'Boy Logic' dictates that if it takes longer to wash up after making something than it takes to make it in the first place, then that's negative time equity!

savoury roulade.

Roulades look great on the table. They work well as a starter or a lunch dish or indeed as part of a buffet.

serves **6-8**

150g raw meat or fish
4 eggs, separated
Salt and freshly ground black pepper
1 x 250g pack cream cheese
Freshly chopped herbs
Filling – choose from variations at the end of the recipe

Here's how to make it...

- Preheat oven to 220°C (200°C if using a fan oven) or Gas Mark 8. Grease and line a baking sheet.
- Place the meat or fish, egg yolks and seasoning into a blender or food processor and whizz until smooth. Transfer to a large clean bowl.
- Whisk up the egg whites until light and foamy in a grease-free bowl. Using a metal spoon, beat a large spoonful of the egg white into the meat or fish and mix to loosen. Gently fold the remaining egg white through.
- Pour into the prepared baking sheet and place in the oven for 7–10 minutes until lightly coloured.

- **2, 3 and 4 Oven Aga,** cook on the 3rd set of runners in the Roasting Oven for 7–10 minutes.
- **Rayburn,** cook on the 4th set of runners in the Main Oven with the Thermodial reading Roast.
- Allow to cool in the baking sheet and turn out onto a large sheet of baking paper on top of a damp tea towel. Spread with filling and roll up onto a plate. Chill before serving.

Variations

Salmon, watercress and ricotta *Use salmon to whizz with the egg yolks. To prepare the filling, whizz 1 bag watercress with 1 tub ricotta.*

Chicken and mushroom *Use chicken fillet to whizz with the egg yolks and prepare the filling by whizzing 200g cream cheese with 200g sautéed mushrooms.*

Cod and lemon *Use cod fillet (skin removed) to whizz with the egg yolks and prepare the filling by mixing the finely grated zest of 2 lemons and the juice of half a lemon with 200g cream cheese.*

James says...

When rolling, it's best to roll away from yourself ensuring the seam is at the base of the rolled roulade.

savoury soufflé.

A soufflé is quick, easy and satisfying, as a starter, main or just to eat on its own.

enough for 4

20g butter, melted
20g finely grated Parmesan, for coating
50g butter
50g plain flour
500ml milk
100g grated cheese, eg Cheddar or Gruyère
6 eggs, separated

Here's how to make it...

- Preheat oven to 180°C (160°C if using a fan oven) or Gas Mark 4.
- Prepare the soufflé dish. Grease the inside with melted butter and cover the inside of the dish with Parmesan.
- Melt the butter in a pan and add the flour. Cook for a few moments until sandy in colour. Remove from heat.
- Add the milk, a little at a time, mixing between each addition. Add cheese and egg yolks and mix well. Heat gently until thickened.
- Whisk egg whites until light and fluffy in a grease-free bowl, then gently fold into the cheese mixture.
- Pour into a soufflé dish and cook for 20–25 minutes.
  Serve immediately.

- **2, 3 and 4 Oven Aga,** place on the grid shelf on the 4th set of runners in the Roasting Oven and cook for 20–25 minutes.
- **Rayburn,** place on the grid shelf on the 5th set of runners in the Main Oven with the Thermodial reading between Bake and Roast for 20–25 minutes.

Variations

Salmon and watercress *Replace the cheese with 150g salmon that's been whizzed up in a blender with a good handful of watercress.*

Lamb and spinach soufflé *Replace the cheese with 200g diced cooked lamb and a good handful of chopped baby leaf spinach.*

Carrot and orange soufflé *Replace the Cheddar cheese with an equal quantity of Red Leicester cheese and add 50g grated carrot as well as the finely grated zest of 1 orange.*

Stilton and walnut soufflé *Replace the Cheddar cheese with an equal weight of Stilton and add 25g chopped walnuts.*

St. Agur and leek soufflé *Replace the Cheddar with an equal weight of St. Agur cheese and 2 sautéed leeks.*

James says...

It's important to have a rough surface on the inside of the soufflé dish to allow the soufflé to climb and form its classic shape.

shepherd's pie.

A great meal to come home to on a cold winter's night.

500g minced lamb
1 large onion, chopped
Salt and freshly ground black pepper
250ml red wine
500ml stock
500–750g potatoes, peeled
Knob butter
2 tbsp milk
1 tbsp cornflour blended with a little water

Here's how to make it...

- Preheat oven to 220°C (200°C if using a fan oven) or Gas Mark 8. Grease a baking sheet.
- Place onion, meat, seasoning and stock into a saucepan. Bring to the boil and simmer for 30 minutes. If using an Aga, after bringing to the boil, place the lid on top and place into the Simmering Oven for 30 minutes.
- Boil the potatoes for 20 minutes in a pan of water, or if using an Aga, bring to the boil, drain, pop the lid on and place into the Simmering Oven for 20 minutes.
- Bring the meat mix back to the boil, blend in cornflour and water and stir continuously until thickened. Pour into a pie dish and set aside to cool.

- Mash the potato with butter and milk. Place on top of the meat mixture and place into the oven for 20 minutes until brown and golden.
- **2, 3 and 4 Oven Aga,** cook on the 3rd set of runners in the Roasting Oven for 7–10 minutes.
- **Rayburn,** cook on the 4th set of runners in the Main Oven with the Thermodial reading Roast.

Variations

Cumberland pie *Make as above, but use minced beef instead of lamb and sprinkle potato with grated cheese and fresh breadcrumbs.*

Cottage pie *Make as above but use minced beef instead of lamb and add 1 diced carrot and 4 tbsp frozen peas into meat mix.*

James says...

It's important to add the cornflour as this will thicken the meat mixture so the potato does not fall into the meat mix.

soup.

Very easy to make and full of home-cooked flavour. Here are two types of soup: broth and purée.

serves **4**

Broth	**Purée**
1 litre beef or vegetable stock	*1 litre chicken or vegetable stock*
150g meat	*25g flour*
1 onion, diced	*1 onion, diced*
1 tsp vegetable oil	*1 tsp vegetable oil*
250g diced vegetables (carrot, turnip, swede, leek, onion, celery)	*750g diced vegetables*
25g barley	*25g butter or margarine*
Bouquet garni	*Bouquet garni*
Salt and freshly ground black pepper	*Salt and freshly ground black pepper*

Here's how to make it...

- To make a broth type soup, place the onion in a pan with the oil and soften. Add the vegetables and all other ingredients, bring to the boil and simmer on a low heat for 25–30 minutes.
- To make a purée type, place the onion in a pan with the butter and cook until soft. Add the other vegetables and cook for a few moments. Add the flour and cook through stirring regularly for about 2 minutes. Add all other ingredients and bring to the boil. Simmer for 25–30 minutes and blend to a smooth purée.

- **2, 3 and 4 Oven Aga,** after bringing to the boil, place the lid on top and place into the Simmering Oven for 25–30 minutes.
- **Rayburn,** after bringing to the boil, place the lid on top and cook in the Lower Oven with the Thermodial reading Bake.

Variations

Potato and pear soup *Using the purée recipe, add 2/3 potatoes to 1/3 pears.*

Butternut squash *Using the purée recipe, prepare a butternut squash reserving the seeds and cook through with 1 tsp cinnamon. Dry the seeds in the oven or toast lightly in a pan to serve on top of the soup.*

James says...

Soup freezes well too.

stuffing.

Roast chicken is not roast chicken without stuffing. Stuffed pork loin is not stuffed pork loin without stuffing. Christmas is not Christmas without stuffing. And it's easy peasy!

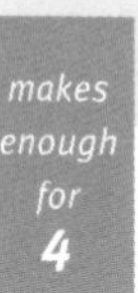

50g fresh breadcrumbs
1 onion, chopped and sautéed in 1 tsp oil
15g butter or margarine, melted
1 tbsp freshly chopped parsley
1 tsp dried mixed herbs
Grated zest of 1/2 lemon
Salt and freshly ground black pepper
1 egg beaten

Here's how to make it...

- Place breadcrumbs into a large baking bowl.
- Add the onion, fat, herbs, seasoning and zest and mix together.
- Add egg to bind the mixture to a stiff consistency.
- Place into the neck end of poultry or middle of pork joint. Alternatively, place into a 500g loaf tin and bake beside the roast.

Variations

Sage and onion *Add 2 tbsp freshly chopped sage or 1 tbsp dried sage.*

Nut and raisin stuffing *Add 50g seedless raisins and 50g chopped nuts to the mix.*

Prune *Add 6 chopped prunes and 25g mixed nuts to the stuffing mix.*

Apple and celery *Chop and sauté 2 sticks of celery in 1 tsp oil and add to the stuffing mix together with 1 small cooking apple, coarsely grated.*

Mushroom *Sauté 50g chopped bacon and 50g chopped mushrooms. Add to the stuffing mix.*

James says...

When making stuffing, always stuff the neck end of poultry and not the cavity. Ensure the stuffing is cooked through as it will always be denser than the meat itself. Use a thermometer to judge, it should reach a minimum of 72°C for a minimum of 2 minutes.

vinaigrette.

Turns a salad into something a lot more interesting.

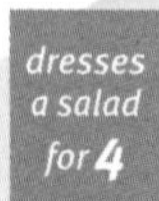

Pinch salt
4 tbsp extra virgin olive oil
2 tbsp vinegar – balsamic, red wine, white wine, rice wine, cider, sherry
1 tsp freshly chopped parsley
½ tsp mustard
A little freshly ground black pepper
1 tsp freshly chopped chives

Here's how to make it...

- Place all of the ingredients into a screw top jar and shake well until mixture appears cloudy.
- Serve and use at once to dress a salad.

Variations

French dressing *4 tbsp extra virgin olive oil, 2 tbsp lemon juice, ¼ tsp caster sugar, ¼ tbsp mustard powder, salt and freshly ground black pepper, few drops of Worcestershire sauce.*

Mix as above.

James says...

When you shake the dressings you make an emulsion of the oil and vinegar. When the jar is rested this will separate out, so if you have some spare ensure you shake it up again before using.

white sauce.

Whether it's to coat, bind or pour over food, sauces are not that difficult, and the most basic is the roux.

makes **250ml** *sauce*

Sauce	Plain Flour	Fat (Butter or Margarine)	Liquid
Pouring	12.5g	12.5g	275ml milk
Coating	25g	25g	275ml milk
Binding	25g	25g	150ml milk
Velouté	25g	25g	75ml milk and 75ml stock

Here's how to make it...

- Melt the fat in a saucepan over a medium heat.
- Add the flour and, using a wooden spoon, beat to form a pale ball. Cook for a few moments until sandy in colour.
- Remove from the heat and add a little of the liquid at a time, beating well until absorbed.
- Bring to the boil, stirring constantly until thickened.

Variations for pouring sauce

Parsley *After thickening add 2 tbsp freshly chopped parsley.*

Cheese *After thickening add 2 tbsp grated mature Cheddar and 1 tbsp English mustard powder.*

Mushroom *Sauté 75g chopped mushrooms in a little oil. When the sauce is thickened, add mushrooms and pan juice and stir through.*

James says...

Sauces only go lumpy if you let them! So keep stirring while adding the liquid and thickening.

sweet.

mix.

crumble. bread. flapjacks.
jam. chocolate sauce.
trifle. crème brûlée.
crème caramel. biscuits.
choux pastry. custard.
syllabub. lemon meringue
pie. meringue. steamed
pudding. sponge. swiss
roll. pavlova. scones. queen
cakes. muffins. shortbread.
sweet shortcrust pastry.
traybake. sweet soufflé.

crumble.

'Everyone is good at cooking something, and I'm good at cooking crumble.' I once heard these lyrics being sung in a pub in London. And it's true, everyone is good at cooking something.

50g plain white flour
25g plain wholemeal flour
50g unsalted butter or margarine
75g soft brown muscovado sugar
25g rolled porridge oats
1 tsp powdered cinnamon
Filling – see variations opposite
50g caster sugar

Here's how to make it...

- Preheat oven to 190°C (170°C if using a fan oven) or Gas Mark 5.
- Mix the flours together in a bowl and rub the fat in.
- Stir through the other ingredients.
- Place a filling from the variations at the end of the recipe into a dish and sprinkle caster sugar on top followed by the crumble mix.
- Place into the centre of the oven for 25 minutes until golden on top.
- **2, 3 and 4 Oven Aga,** cook on the 4th set of runners in the Roasting Oven for 15 minutes adding the cold plain shelf on top for 10 minutes.
- **Rayburn,** cook on the 4th set of runners in the Main Oven with the Thermodial reading Bake for 25 minutes.

Variations

Apple and blackberry *700g peeled apples and 250g blackberries.*

Plum *750g plums, cut in half with stones removed.*

Cherry *1kg fresh stoned cherries or 1kg tinned cherries, drained.*

Rhubarb and orange *Mix 700g sliced rhubarb and 1 tin mandarin oranges, drained.*

James says...

To make a savoury crumble, or a crunchy topping for vegetables, use the crumble topping recipe above but omit the sugar and cinnamon and add 1 tsp dried herbs or herbs de provence.

bread.

The smell of freshly cooked bread is really inviting. I often make bread if I'm feeling cross with someone, as the kneading process is great for getting rid of anger.

250g strong plain flour
15g butter or margarine
1 tsp salt
150ml water, at body temperature
1 x 7g sachet dried yeast.

Here's how to make it...

- Sieve flour and salt into a mixing bowl and using your fingertips, rub the fat into the flour until it looks like very fine breadcrumbs. Give the bowl a gentle shake to bring any fat that's not rubbed in to the surface.
- Stir in the yeast and add the water, mixing to form a ball of dough.
- Turn out onto a floured board and knead well by lifting one end of the dough and rubbing it heavily over the other end with the palm of the hand. Repeat this process for 5 minutes. The dough will appear and feel smooth.
- Place the dough back into the bowl, cover with a damp tea towel and leave in a warm place, such as an airing cupboard or next to an Aga or Rayburn. After about 40 minutes the dough will have doubled in size.
- Preheat oven to 250°C (230°C if using a fan oven) or Gas Mark 8.
- Making a fist with your hand, thump the dough. It will collapse. Turn out onto a floured board and knead for another 5 minutes.

- Place into a loaf tin and leave to rise for 20 minutes. Bake in the oven for 35–40 minutes until golden brown and the bottom sounds hollow when tapped.
- Cool on a wire rack.
- **2, 3 and 4 Oven Aga**, cook on the floor of the Roasting Oven for 35–40 minutes.
- **Rayburn**, cook on the floor of the Main Oven with the Thermodial reading Roast for 35–40 minutes.

Variations

Wholemeal bread *Substitute white flour for wholemeal flour in the recipe above.*

Milk bread *Substitute milk for water and glaze loaf with beaten egg before baking.*

Currant bread *Add 25g caster sugar and 50g currants to mix above after rubbing fat into flour. Brush top of loaf with beaten egg before baking.*

James says...

Ensure the liquid is at blood temperature to allow the yeast to work. If it's any hotter the yeast will die. You can tell water is at blood temperature when you put your finger in it and it feels neither hot nor cold.

flapjacks.

Great after-school treats.

makes
8

75g brown sugar
75g butter
2 tbsp golden syrup
125g rolled oats

Here's how to make it...

- Preheat oven to 170°C (150°C if using a fan oven) or Gas Mark 3. Grease an 18cm square shallow tin.
- Melt the sugar, fat and syrup together in a pan until sugar is dissolved.
- Add oats and mix through.
- Spread into tin and press firmly. Bake for 15–20 minutes until golden brown.
- When cooked, cut into 2 x 6cm fingers and allow to cool in tin. When cooled, remove from tin.
- **2 Oven Aga,** cook on the 4th set of runners in the Roasting Oven for 15–20 minutes with the cold plain shelf above.
- **3 and 4 Oven Aga,** cook on the 4th set of runners in the Baking Oven for 15–20 minutes.
- **Rayburn,** cook on the 4th set of runners in the Main Oven with the Thermodial reading Bake.

Variations

Cherry flapjacks *Add 50g chopped glace cherries to the mixture when adding the oats.*

Fruit flapjacks *Add 50g currants or dried mixed fruit to the mixture when adding the oats.*

Nut and seeds *Add 50g nut and seed mix to the mixture when adding the oats.*

James says...

Ensure all of the sugar has dissolved to prevent the mix from going grainy.

jam.

Growing up on the farm, Mum made vast quantities of jam every year. It's such an economical way of preserving fruit.

1½ kg fruit

1½ kg preserving sugar

To each 1½ kg of fruit add the following amount of water:

- *Apricots–250ml*
- *Blackberry and apple–250ml*
- *Plum–250ml*
- *Blackberries–600ml*
- *Blackcurrants–1½ litres*
- *Raspberries and strawberries–none, but add pectin*

Here's how to make it...

- Wash and prepare the fruit. It's best to use fruit that isn't bruised but is nice and ripe.
- Place the fruit into a preserving pan or large heavy-bottomed saucepan with the water, and heat gently until softened. Add the sugar and cook until dissolved.
- Bring to the boil. Boil rapidly for about 20 minutes until setting point is reached. To test place a tsp of jam on a cold plate and place in the fridge. After 5 minutes push the jam with your finger. If it wrinkles, the jam has reached setting point.
- Pour into clean dry jars, cover and allow to cool.

James says...

Soft fruit like strawberries and raspberries do not contain any pectin – the setting agent naturally found in harder fruits. Pectin can be purchased in supermarkets and is commercially called 'Certo'.

chocolate sauce.

Use for all manner of puddings as a sauce or as a sweet fondue. Or, eat it on its own!

makes enough for **4 - 6**

150g bar plain or milk chocolate
3 tbsp milk
1 tsp vanilla extract

Here's how to make it...

- Break the chocolate into pieces and place into a microwave bowl.
- Add the other ingredients and microwave on medium power for 3 minutes. Stir through.
- If using an Aga or Rayburn, place bowl on a piece of kitchen paper on the enamel on top of the cooker for 10 minutes to melt. Stir through.

Variations

Chocolate orange sauce *Add finely grated zest of 1 orange.*

Honey chocolate sauce *Add 1 tbsp runny honey.*

James says...

Never put chocolate into a saucepan and place on the hob as it will seize and burn.

trifle.

The sherry is optional, but I believe it helps the overall trifle experience.

4 sponge cakes or stale cake
1 tbsp jam
125ml fruit syrup or sherry
Tin of fruit cocktail
250ml thick custard (see recipe 36, page 70)
150ml double cream
Chopped nuts for decoration

Here's how to make it...

- Split the sponge cakes and spread with jam. Cut into small pieces. Place into a glass dish.
- Pour the sherry over the sponge and leave to soak for at least 1 hour.
- Drain the fruit and place on top of the sponge. Pour the custard over the fruit and leave till cold.
- Whip the cream and spread over the trifle, or pipe if you're feeling adventurous.
- Decorate with nuts and keep in the refrigerator until required.

James says...

Use a good sweet cream sherry in this, not a dry one.

crème brûlée.

One of those classic desserts that needs nothing else added.

serves 6

600ml double cream
1 vanilla pod, split down the middle and seeds set aside or 1 tsp vanilla extract
4 large egg yolks
125g caster sugar

Here's how to make it...

- Preheat oven to 150°C (130°C if using a fan oven) or Gas Mark 2.
- Pour the cream into a saucepan, add the vanilla pod and seeds or the extract and bring slowly to the boil. Set aside and allow to infuse for about 30 minutes.
- Place the egg yolks into a bowl and add the caster sugar. Whisk until light and fluffy. Add a little of the milk and whisk, add the remainder of the milk and mix together, discarding the vanilla pod.
- Pour back into the saucepan and heat gently, whisking continuously for 2–3 minutes on a low heat. Pour into 6 individual ramekins and set into a deep-sided roasting tray. Pour hot water into the tray so the water comes half way up the sides of the ramekins. Place into the oven for 30–35 minutes. Refrigerate overnight.

- **2, 3 and 4 Oven Aga,** cook on the 4th set of runners in the Roasting Oven with the cold plain shelf on top for 20 minutes.
- **Rayburn,** cook on the 4th set of runners in the Main Oven with the Thermodial reading between Bake and Roast for 25 minutes.
- Scatter 2 tsp of caster sugar over the top of the chilled brûlée and melt with a kitchen blow torch.

James says...

It's important to add the water to the roasting tray so the custard cooks at a moderate temperature and slowly.

crème caramel.

A classic dessert, perfect for finishing off Sunday lunch or a dinner party.

serves
6

175g granulated sugar
600ml double cream
1 vanilla pod, split down the middle and seeds set aside or 1 tsp vanilla extract
4 eggs
4 egg yolks
50g caster sugar

Here's how to make it...

- Preheat oven to 170°C (150°C if using a fan oven) or Gas Mark 3. Warm 6 ramekins in the oven.
- Pour the granulated sugar into a heavy-based pan and gently heat until dissolved. Increase the heat and boil rapidly until the syrup turns a rich golden brown, caramel colour. Set the base of the pan into cold water to immediately stop the cooking. Divide the syrup between 6 ramekins.
- Pour the cream into a saucepan, add the vanilla pod and seeds or the extract and bring slowly to the boil.
- Place the eggs and egg yolks into a bowl and add the caster sugar, whisk until light and fluffy. Add a little of the milk and whisk, then add the remainder of the milk and mix together, discarding the vanilla pod.

- Pour back into the saucepan and heat gently, whisking continuously for 2–3 minutes on a gentle heat. Pour into 6 individual ramekins and set into a deep-sided roasting tray. Pour hot water into the tray so the water comes halfway up the sides of the ramekins. Place into the oven for 30–35 minutes. Refrigerate overnight.
- **2, 3 and 4 Oven Aga,** cook on the 4th set of runners in the Roasting Oven with the cold plain shelf on top for 20 minutes.
- **Rayburn,** cook on the 4th set of runners in the Main Oven with the Thermodial reading between Bake and Roast for 25 minutes.
- To turn out, dip a table knife in boiling water and carefully run around the edges of the crème. Place a serving dish over the top and invert, remove the ramekin.

James says...

This mixture is different to the crème brûlée as the extra egg yolk and egg whites will allow it to set to become more of a wobbly custard.

biscuits.

Crunchy, crumbly, scrummy – there's nothing a boy likes more than a homemade biscuit. Go on, put the kettle on...

makes **12**

100g plain flour, sifted
50g butter or margarine
50g caster sugar
½ egg, beaten
Caster sugar or icing sugar for sprinkling

Here's how to make it...

- Preheat oven to 180°C (160°C if using a fan oven) or Gas Mark 4. Grease a baking sheet.
- Using your fingertips, rub the fat into the flour until it looks like breadcrumbs. Give the bowl a gentle shake to bring any fat that's not rubbed in to the surface.
- Add the sugar and mix.
- Mix to a very stiff dough with the egg. Knead until smooth.
- Roll out thinly on a floured board. Cut into shapes and prick the top with a fork.
- Place onto a baking tray and bake for 10–15 minutes until firm and lightly golden.
- Cool on a wire rack. Sprinkle with caster or icing sugar.

- **2 Oven Aga,** cook on the 4th set of runners in the Roasting Oven for 10–12 minutes with the cold plain shelf above.
- **3 and 4 Oven Aga,** cook on the 3rd set of runners in the Baking Oven for 10–15 minutes.
- **Rayburn,** cook on the 4th set of runners in the Main Oven with the Thermodial reading Bake.

Variations

Fruit biscuits *Mix in 50g currants when adding the sugar.*

Coconut biscuits *Add 50g desiccated coconut to the mix when adding the sugar.*

Cherry biscuits *Mix in 50g chopped glacé cherries when adding the sugar.*

Chocolate biscuits *Replace 1 tbsp of the flour with 1 tbsp cocoa powder.*

Ginger biscuits *Add 1 tsp dried ginger to the mix when adding the sugar.*

James says...

Less is more when cooking biscuits as they will continue to firm up when they come out of the oven.

choux pastry.

Use this pastry for profiteroles, éclairs or gougère.

makes 10 eclairs 10cm long or 15 profiteroles	*140ml water* *55g butter* *65g plain flour, sifted* *2 eggs, beaten*

Here's how to make it...

- Place the water and butter into a saucepan and heat gently until the butter is melted. Bring to the boil.
- Add the flour to the boiling liquid, beating over the heat until the mixture comes away from the sides of the pan and forms a smooth ball. Remove from the heat and allow to cool slightly.
- Beat in one egg at a time, until you have a shiny mixture that easily stretches from the spoon when lifted.
- For éclairs, place into a piping bag and pipe lines onto a baking tray lined with greaseproof paper in well spaced apart 10cm lines. For profiteroles, pipe balls of about 5cm in diameter on a tray lined with greaseproof paper. For a gougère, place onto a tray lined with greaseproof paper in a large circle and fill the middle with a savoury filling.
- To cook, place into a preheated oven at 220°C (200°C if using a fan oven) or Gas Mark 8 for 30–40 minutes until golden brown and crisp. Do not open the oven door for the first 30 minutes.

- **2, 3 and 4 Oven Aga,** cook on the 3rd set of runners in the Roasting Oven for 30 minutes.
- **Rayburn,** cook on the 4th set of runners in the Main Oven with the Thermodial reading between Bake and Roast for 30 minutes.
- For éclairs and profiteroles, cut a small hole in the side and remove the gooey filling. Pipe in some freshly whipped cream and cover the top in melted chocolate.

Variations

Cheese choux *Add 55g of grated mature Cheddar cheese and 1 tsp English mustard powder to the mix after beating in the egg and mix to combine.*

Chocolate choux *Substitute 25g of the flour in the recipe above for 25g sieved cocoa powder.*

Herb *Add 1 tbsp freshly chopped herbs to the choux after beating in the eggs. Mix thoroughly.*

James says...

It's the water in choux pastry that makes it rise so it's important not to boil it too much.

custard.

Technically a custard is a hot or cold mixture set or thickened with egg yolks. Whatever! It tastes great when made fresh. Have a go, it's not that difficult.

enough to serve **4**

250ml milk
1 tsp vanilla extract or seeds from a fresh vanilla pod
3 egg yolks
150g caster sugar

Here's how to make it....

- Gently heat the milk with vanilla extract or vanilla seeds in a pan until it just comes to the boil and no more. Remove from heat.
- In a bowl, whisk together the egg yolks and sugar until light and fluffy.
- Add a little bit of the hot milk to the egg mix and whisk well. Add the remaining milk and whisk to combine.
- Pour back into the pan and whisk over a medium heat until thickened.

Variations

Lemon custard *When warming the milk, add the grated zest of 2 lemons to the milk while heating. (This recipe is with thanks to Caroline Korshak, manager of the Aga Cook Shop in Knightsbridge.)*

Orange custard *Add 1 tbsp Grand Marnier to the custard after thickening and mix through.*

Crème pâtissière *Whisk the egg yolks with 2 tbsp plain flour and (for custard tarts) 2 tbsp corn flour before adding the milk.*

James says...

In 1844 Alfred Bird developed Bird's Custard powder because his wife was allergic to eggs – a key ingredient in custard. On a trivial note, Alfred's son, also called Alfred (funny that!), still holds the record of cycling a tricycle from Land's End to John O'Groats. Bird's Custard fed our boys during World War I but was rationed during World War 2. If you must use it, refer to the back of the tin for directions on how to reconstitute it.

syllabub.

A cream for adults. It's boozy, so be careful if driving.

4 tbsp caster sugar
150ml white wine – Pinot Grigio is good
4–5 tbsp Grand Marnier
Grated zest of 1 lemon
600ml double cream

Here's how to make it...

- Place all of the ingredients except the cream into a saucepan and heat gently until the sugar is dissolved. Cool completely.
- Pour in the cream and whisk using an electric mixer until soft peaks result.
- Chill in the refrigerator until firm.
- Serve with desserts or brandy snaps.

Variations

Christmas syllabub *Add the grated zest of 1 orange, and 1 tsp mixed spice.*

Raspberry syllabub *Add 150g good quality raspberry jam.*

Lemon syllabub *Replace Grand Marnier with Limoncello.*

James says...

This will take longer to whisk than ordinary cream due to the amount of liquid. However, stick at it as the mixture may curdle if left unattended.

lemon meringue pie.

Tangy and sweet.

1 quantity sweet shortcrust pastry (see recipe 48, page 92)
1 quantity meringue (see recipe 39, page 74)
25g cornflour
125ml water
15g butter or margarine
Finely grated zest and juice of 2 lemons
50g caster sugar
2 egg yolks

Here's how to make it...

- Preheat oven to 220°C (200°C if using a fan oven) or Gas Mark 7.
- Bake the pastry blind in a quiche dish.
- Mix together the cornflour and water and pour into a saucepan. Add the fat and the juice and zest of the lemons. Add the caster sugar. Bring to the boil stirring continuously. Allow to cool slightly. Beat in egg yolks.
- Pour the lemon mixture on top of the pastry. Top with the meringue mix.
- Place into the centre of the oven for 10–15 minutes until golden on top.
- **2, 3 and 4 Oven Aga,** cook on the 4th set of runners in the Roasting Oven for 15 minutes.
- **Rayburn,** cook on the 4th set of runners in the Main Oven with the Thermodial reading mid-point between Bake and Roast for 15 minutes.

James says...

It's important to mix the cornflour with the cold water as it prevents the filling from going lumpy.

39

meringue.

Meringues. Gooey and chewy. Mmm mmm...

makes 6 or 6 6cm baskets

4 egg whites, at room temperature
225g caster sugar, sieved

Here's how to make it...

- Preheat oven to 110°C (100°C if using a fan oven) or Gas Mark ¼.
- Place the egg whites into a clean, grease-free bowl and whisk using an electric mixer (with the balloon whisk attachment) until nice and foamy. You know they are ready when you can turn the bowl upside down and they don't fall out. *Don't try this at home. I lost the plot once at a cookery demonstration, put the bowl above my head and everything fell out. What a mess! Mind you, my hair was nice and shiny for days!*
- With the mixer running at full speed, pour in the caster sugar in a steady stream. The mixture will go shiny and when you lift the whisk out stiff peaks should be visible.
- Decide what shape of meringue you want, and either pipe or use a spoon to place the mixture on a baking tray lined with greaseproof paper. Keep the meringues well spaced apart.
- Place the meringues into the oven for 2–3 hours until crisp and well dried out.
- **2, 3 and 4 Oven Aga,** place into the Roasting Oven on the 4th set of runners for 2 minutes and then place into the Simmering Oven for 1½ hours.
- **Rayburn,** place onto the 5th set of runners in the Main Oven with the Thermodial reading Roast for 2 minutes and move to the Lower Oven

for 30 minutes. Can also be cooked on the low or idling position (120°C) runner 5 for about 2 hours.

- Remove the meringues from the greaseproof paper and place onto a wire rack to cool.

Variations

Italian meringues *Place the egg whites and sugar into a bowl on top of a pan of gently simmering water. Whisk until the mixture leaves a very thick trail across the surface when the beaters are lifted. Remove the bowl from the heat and continue to whisk for 2 minutes until cooled.*

Brown sugar meringues *Using the mixture and method above, add 25g brown sugar. The meringues will turn out a nice caramel colour.*

Meringue cuite *This is a great mix for meringue baskets. Replace the caster sugar with icing sugar and place it with the egg whites into a bowl on top of a pan of gently simmering water. Whisk until the mixture leaves a very thick trail across the surface when the beaters are lifted. Remove the bowl from the heat and continue to whisk for 2 minutes until cooled.*

James says...

Never bake with eggs that are just out of the fridge. Making meringues is all about beating in air. Eggs will incorporate more air if at room temperature. I learnt that from watching the film Calendar Girls. Thank you Women's Institute!

steamed pudding.

Really worth the effort. This is nice and easy and great with custard.

100g butter or margarine, softened
100g caster sugar
2 eggs
150g self-raising flour
2 tbsp milk

Filling – choose from variations opposite

Here's how to make it...

- Grease a pudding basin and a piece of foil or greaseproof paper.
- Place all of the ingredients into a large bowl and mix together with a wooden spoon.
- Place your chosen filling from the variations at the end of the recipe into the bottom of the basin and place your mixed ingredients on top.
- Fold a pleat into the foil or greaseproof paper and set on top of the basin. Tie around with string.
- Set the basin on top of an upturned saucer in a large saucepan. Fill up to half the height of the basin with water and bring to the boil. Place the lid on the pan and steam for 2 hours, topping up water as required. Turn out onto a plate and enjoy.

- **2, 3 and 4 Oven Aga,** cook in the Simmering Oven for 2 hours after rapidly boiling on the Boiling Plate for 5 minutes.
- **Rayburn,** cook in the Main Oven for 2 hours after rapidly boiling on top for 5 minutes with the Thermodial reading Bake.

Variations

Jam *Add 6 large tbsp jam to basin before adding sponge mix.*

Apple and ginger *Core and peel 2 cooking apples and gently stew in a saucepan with 4 tbsp caster sugar and a little grated ginger. Add to basin before adding sponge mix.*

Golden syrup *Add 4 tbsp golden syrup to the basin before adding the sponge mix.*

James says...

It's important to bring the pudding to a good boil before simmering and to top up the water during the cooking process as it's the steam that cooks the pudding.

sponge.

Also called a Victoria sandwich.

makes a cake for **8**

100g butter or margarine, softened
100g caster sugar
2 eggs, beaten
100g self-raising flour, sieved

Here's how to make it...

- Preheat oven to 180°C (160°C if using a fan oven) or Gas Mark 5. Grease and line the inside of two 15cm sandwich tins.
- Cream the fat and sugar together with a wooden spoon or mixer until the mixture is white and fluffy and it drops off the spoon to the count of two.
- Add a third of the egg at a time and beat into the creamed mixture.
- Fold the flour into the mixture.
- Divide between the 2 tins and place into the middle of the oven for 20–25 minutes. It's ready when the edges have come away from the sides of the tin and the cake springs back when gently pressed.
- **2 Oven Aga,** cook on the 4th set of runners in the Roasting Oven with the cold plain shelf on the 2nd set of runners for 20–25 minutes.
- **3 and 4 Oven Aga,** cook on the 4th set of runners in the Baking Oven.
- **Rayburn,** cook on the 4th set of runners in the Main Oven with the Thermodial reading Bake.
- Allow to cool in the tin for a few moments. Turn onto a wire rack to cool. Sandwich together with jam or cream and fruit.

Variations

Chocolate victoria sandwich *Replace 50g of flour for 50g sifted cocoa powder.*

Almond victoria sandwich *Add 2 tbsp ground almonds to the flour.*

Genoese *After folding in the flour, add 2 tbsp of melted butter and fold through.*

James says...

To get a really good rise, warm the sugar and flour for a few moments in the oven at 100°C Gas Mark 1/4 before baking or in a bowl sitting on top of an Aga or Rayburn.

swiss roll.

A quick and easy light sponge that can be rolled up to make a swiss roll or baked in a cake tin to make a very light cake.

2 eggs at room temperature
50g caster sugar
50g plain flour
jam

Here's how to make it...

- Preheat oven to 220°C (200°C if using a fan oven) or Gas Mark 7. Grease and line the inside of a swiss roll tin (18 x 30cm).
- Crack the eggs into the mixer bowl, add the sugar and whisk on high speed for 5–10 minutes until the mixture has risen. Try writing your name in the mixture with the whisk attachment – if it stays visible for a few seconds it's ready!
- Carefully fold the flour into the mixture with a metal spoon.
- Pour into the swiss roll tin and place in the middle of the oven for 7–10 minutes. The swiss roll is ready when the edges of the cake have come away from the sides of the tin. The sponge should spring back when gently pressed.
- **2, 3 and 4 Oven Aga,** cook on the grid shelf placed on the floor of the Roasting Oven for 7 minutes.
- **Rayburn,** cook on the 4th set of runners in the Main Oven with the Thermodial reading Bake.

- Allow to cool in the tin for a few moments before turning out onto a sugared piece of greaseproof paper that is placed on top of a damp tea towel. Turn the swiss roll over, remove the greaseproof paper and cut off the edges. Spread with warmed jam and roll up.

Variations

Chocolate swiss roll *Replace 1 tbsp flour for 1 tbsp sifted cocoa powder. Fill with whipped cream and fruit.*

Lemon swiss roll *Fold in the finely grated zest of 1 lemon when adding flour to the mixture. To fill, spread with 300 ml whipped double cream with 2 tbsp of lemon curd folded into it.*

James says...

When rolling, always roll away from yourself to help ensure the seam of the swiss roll ends up on the bottom.

pavlova.

A fluffy cloud topped with cream and fruit. Easier than you think!

makes **1** for 6–8 to share

6 egg whites, at room temperature
A pinch of salt
350g caster sugar, sieved
½ tsp vanilla extract
1 tbsp white wine vinegar
1 tsp cornflour
300ml double cream, whipped
Fresh fruit of your choice

Here's how to make it...

- Preheat oven to 110°C (100°C if using a fan oven) or Gas Mark ¼.
- Place the egg whites into a clean grease-free bowl and whisk as in the meringue recipe (see page 72).
- With the mixer running at full steam, pour in the caster sugar in a steady stream. The mixture will go shiny and when the beaters are removed stiff peaks will be visible. Now add the vanilla extract, white wine vinegar and cornflour, turn the mixer back on and mix fast for a few seconds.
- Draw a circle onto a piece of greaseproof paper. Turn the paper upside down and spread the mixture to the edges of the circle.
- Place the pavlova into the oven for 2–3 hours until crisp and well dried out.
- **2, 3 and 4 Oven Aga,** place into the Roasting Oven on the 4th set of runners for 2 minutes and then place into the Simmering Oven for 1 ½ hours.

- **Rayburn,** place onto the 5th set of runners in the Main Oven with the Thermodial reading Roast for 2 minutes and move to the Lower Oven for 1 ½ hours.
- Remove the pavlova from the greaseproof paper and place onto a wire rack to cool.
- Decorate with freshly whipped cream and some fruit. Yummy.

Variations

Dacquise *A French name for a hazelnut meringue. After mixing, carefully fold in 50g chopped hazelnuts with a large metal spoon. Cook as above.*

James says...

To crack or not to crack? Pavlovas do crack when removed from greaseproof paper – it's all part of the charm. Perhaps that's why we add cream?

scones.

Scones are quick and easy to make and take no time at all to cook. The secret to good scones is not to roll them – use the palm of your hand to spread out the dough.

makes **10** 6 cm scones

250g self-raising flour
½ level tsp salt
1 level tsp baking powder
50g butter or margarine
125ml milk
1 egg, beaten (for glazing)

Here's how to make it...

- Preheat oven to 220°C (200°C if using a fan oven) or Gas Mark 8. Grease a baking sheet.
- Sieve the flour, salt and baking powder into a mixing bowl.
- Using your fingertips, rub the fat into the flour until it looks like breadcrumbs. Give the bowl a gentle shake to bring any fat that's not rubbed in to the surface.
- Make a well in the centre of the bowl with a palate knife and add half the milk. Mix together, then stir in the remaining milk and mix to form a dough.
- Turn out onto a lightly floured surface and knead for a few moments until the dough is smooth.
- Push down on the dough with your palm to spread it out. Lightly flour a fluted 6cm scone cutter and press into the dough. Repeat across the dough, cutting the shapes as tightly together as possible. Re-roll excess dough and cut out more scones.

- Place the scones onto the baking sheet and brush the top with beaten egg. Bake for 7–10 minutes. You'll know they're cooked if you hear a hollow sound when you tap the bottom. Remove from the oven, place on a cooling rack and cover with a clean tea towel.
- **2, 3 and 4 Oven Aga,** cook on the 3rd set of runners in the Roasting Oven for 7–10 minutes.
- **Rayburn,** cook on the 2nd set of runners in the Main Oven with the Thermodial reading Roast.

Variations

Cherry scones *Add 50g chopped glace cherries to the mixture before adding the milk.*

Fruit scones *Add 50g currants to the mixture before adding the milk.*

Walnut scones *Add 50g chopped walnuts to the mixture before adding the milk.*

Cheese scones *Add 50g grated Cheddar and 1 tsp English mustard powder to the mixture before adding the milk. Sprinkle some grated Cheddar on top instead of brushing with egg and use a straight sided scone cutter.*

James says...

Don't add too much flour to the work top as this will make the scones tough.

queen cakes.

Quick, easy and great for lunchboxes. Oooh... and good with a cuppa too.

50g butter or margarine, softened
50g caster sugar
75g self-raising flour
1 egg, beaten

Here's how to make it...

- Preheat oven to 180°C (160°C if using a fan oven) or Gas Mark 5. Place 12 bun cases into a bun or paté tin.
- Cream the fat and sugar together with a wooden spoon or mixer until the mixture is white and fluffy and it drops off the spoon to the count of two.
- Beat the egg into the creamed mixture.
- Fold the flour into the mixture.
- Divide between the 12 cases, approximately 2 tsp each.
- Place into the middle of the oven for 15–20 minutes. The cakes are ready when they spring back when gently pressed.

- **2 Oven Aga,** cook on the 4th set of runners in the Roasting Oven with the cold plain shelf on the 2nd set of runners for 15–20 minutes.
- **3 and 4 Oven Aga,** cook on the 4th set of runners in the Baking Oven for 15–20 minutes.
- **Rayburn,** cook on the 4th set of runners in the Main Oven with the Thermodial reading Bake for 15–20 minutes.
- Remove from the tin and leave on a wire rack to cool. Decorate with dusted icing sugar.

Variations

Chocolate *Replace 1 tbsp flour with 1 tbsp sifted cocoa powder.*

Coffee *Add 2 tsp coffee essence when folding in the flour.*

Cherry *Add 25g chopped glace cherries after the egg.*

Fruit *Add 25g sultanas or currants after the egg.*

Coconut *Add 25g desiccated coconut with the flour.*

James says...

Why not ice the top by mixing 2 tbsp icing sugar with 2 tsp water and cover with chocolate sprinkles?

muffins.

A very easy, quick, all-in-one muffin mix.

makes **10-12**

250g self raising flour
2 tsp baking powder
100g caster sugar
250ml milk
1 large egg
90ml vegetable oil
Filling – choose from variations opposite

Here's how to make it...

- Preheat oven to 180°C (160°C if using a fan oven) or Gas Mark 4. Place the muffin cases into a muffin tray.
- Place all of the ingredients apart from the filling into a bowl and mix to form a smooth batter.
- Gently fold in the filling.
- Place into the oven for 20–25 minutes until nicely risen and golden on top. Allow to cool slightly and enjoy.
- **2 Oven Aga,** cook on the 4th set of runners in the Roasting Oven for 20–25 minutes with the cold plain shelf on top.
- **3 and 4 Oven Aga,** cook on the 4th set of runners in the Baking Oven for 20–25 minutes.
- **Rayburn,** cook on the 4th set of runners in the Main Oven with the Thermodial reading Bake for 20–25 minutes.

Variations

Blueberry *Add 150g fresh blueberries to the mix.*

Raspberry and white chocolate *Add 150g raspberries and 150g white chocolate chips to the mix.*

Lemon *Add finely grated zest of 2 lemons to the mix.*

Double chocolate *Swap 50g flour for 50g cocoa powder. Add 150g plain chocolate chips to the mix.*

James says...

These are best eaten within 24 hours, but they do freeze well.

shortbread.

Warm biscuits are yummy when they come out of the oven. Compare the cost of these to bought biscuits and I'm sure you'll be amazed.

makes **12** slices

100g plain flour
50g rice flour, or semolina or cornflour
50g caster sugar
100g butter
Caster sugar or icing sugar for sprinkling

Here's how to make it...

- Preheat oven to 170°C (150°C if using a fan oven) or Gas Mark 3. Grease a baking sheet.
- Sieve the flours and caster sugar into a mixing bowl.
- Using your fingertips, rub the butter into the flour until it looks like breadcrumbs. Give the bowl a gentle shake to bring any butter that's not rubbed in to the surface. Knead lightly.
- Shape the dough into an oblong 1cm thick.
- Cut fingers, approximately 3 x 8cm. Place on baking sheet.
- Bake for 20–25 minutes until firm and a pale golden colour.
- Cool on a wire rack, sprinkle with caster or icing sugar.

- **2 Oven Aga,** cook on the 4th set of runners in the Roasting Oven for 20–25 minutes with the cold plain shelf above.
- **3 and 4 Oven Aga,** cook on the 3rd set of runners in the Baking Oven for 20–25 minutes.
- **Rayburn,** cook on the 4th set of runners in the Main Oven with the Thermodial reading Bake.

James says...

If shortbread is allowed to cook too much it will have a bitter flavour. Stick to the cooking times above and all will be ok.

sweet shortcrust pastry.

A great pastry for tarts and sweet flans.

*Lines **1** pie dish or **4** smaller individual ones*

200g plain flour, sieved
½ level tsp salt
1 tbsp caster sugar
100g butter or margarine, cut into small cubes, chilled
1 egg yolk
1 tbsp cold water

Here's how to make it...

- Place the flour, salt and sugar into a bowl. Add the fat and rub in. To rub in, take a little of the flour and some butter in your hands and press it between your thumb and small finger, moving your thumb up through all of your fingers. Repeat until the mixture looks like fine bread crumbs. Alternatively, place fat and flour into a food processor and blitz for a few seconds until it looks like fine bread crumbs.
- Add egg yolk and water and mix together using a table knife. Knead lightly and place into the fridge to rest for 20 minutes before rolling out.
- If baking blind to make a pastry case, bake at 200°C (180°C if using a fan oven) or Gas Mark 7. Place some greaseproof paper over the pastry and fill with baking beans or rice before cooking. After 15 minutes remove paper to colour the pastry. There's no need to bake blind if using an Aga or Rayburn providing the pastry is in a flat bottomed dish on the floor of the Aga Roasting Oven or the floor of the Rayburn Main Oven with the Thermodial reading Roast. Just add the liquid filling to the raw pastry.

Variations

Almond *Add ½ tsp almond essence.*

Lemon *Add grated zest of 1 lemon to flour.*

Chocolate *Replace 25g of the flour with 25g sieved cocoa powder.*

James says...

It's always important to let pastry rest before rolling as the protein in the flour, called gluten, needs to rest. It's a bit like muscles in the body having to rest after working in the gym. If using pastry to make a tart or flan, allow the pastry to hang over the edge of the dish during cooking to minimise shrinkage. Cut excess pastry off with a breadknife before serving.

traybake.

A quick way to make something exciting to accompany a cuppa, rather famous in Northern Ireland. I've been to many parts of the world and only the Northern Irish embrace traybakes – my mum has hundreds of varieties. Also called a sheetcake in the USA.

225g butter or margarine, softened
225g caster sugar
300g self-raising flour, sifted
2 tsp baking powder
4 eggs
2 tbsp milk
Flavouring, select from variations opposite

Topping:
4 tbsp demerara sugar

Here's how to make it...

- Preheat oven to 180°C (160°C if using a fan oven) or Gas Mark 5. Line a deep sided baking tray with greaseproof paper.
- Place all of the ingredients into a mixer and mix well until there's no visible traces of butter. Pour into the prepared tray and sprinkle with sugar.
- Bake in the middle of the oven for 20–30 minutes until a skewer comes out clean when inserted.
- **2 Oven Aga,** cook on the 4th set of runners in the Roasting Oven with the cold plain shelf on the 2nd set of runners for 20–30 minutes.
- **3 and 4 Oven Aga,** cook on the 4th set of runners in the Baking Oven for 20–30 minutes.
- **Rayburn,** cook on the 4th set of runners in the Main Oven with the Thermodial reading Bake for 20–30 minutes.
- Remove from the tin and leave on a wire rack to cool. Slice and enjoy.

Variations

Fruit *Add 300g dried mixed fruit to mix.*

Chocolate orange and pecan *Replace 50g of the flour with 50g sieved cocoa powder. Also add grated zest of an orange and 100g chopped pecans*

Cherry *Add 100g chopped glace cherries.*

St Clements *Add grated rind of 1 lemon, 1 orange and 1 lime and 100g chopped mixed candied peel.*

Lime and coconut *Add 100g desiccated coconut, grated zest of 2 limes and juice of 1 lime.*

James says...

I love all-in-one mixtures like this. Go on! You've no excuse not to, really!

sweet soufflé.

Quite yummy. Make the night before to allow it to set. Traditional recipes use gelatine, but I've come up with an easier version using a lemon jelly. Clever boy, James!

285ml milk
1 vanilla pod, split lengthways, seeds scooped out
4 egg yolks
55g caster sugar
Flavouring – choose from variations opposite
135g pack lemon jelly, melted
300ml double cream, whipped

Here's how to make it...

- Prepare the soufflé dish by tying a length of greaseproof paper around the outside of the dish to make a band that sits 5–6cm above the top of the dish.
- Place the milk and vanilla into a pan and heat to just short of the boil. Allow to cool slightly.
- Whisk the egg yolks and sugar together in a bowl until light and fluffy. Pour in a little of the milk and whisk thoroughly. Add remaining milk and whisk until thickened.
- Allow to cool gently and add your chosen flavouring. Fold in the jelly and cream.
- Place into a soufflé dish and chill overnight in refrigerator.
- Remove band and serve.

Variations

Christmas soufflé *Mix 25g chopped mixed dried fruit, 2 tbsp Grand Marnier, 1 tbsp Drambuie and 1 tsp mixed spice with jelly.*

Strawberry soufflé *Puree 25g fresh strawberries and 1 tbsp Crème de Fraise and mix with jelly. A strawberry jelly can be used instead of lemon.*

Orange soufflé *Add the grated zest and juice of 2 oranges and 2 tbsp Grand Marnier to jelly. An orange jelly can be used instead of lemon.*

Raspberry soufflé *Puree 25g fresh raspberries and 2 tbsp Grand Marnier (or Chambord – a raspberry liqueur) to the jelly. A raspberry jelly can be used instead of lemon.*

Lemon soufflé *Add grated zest and juice of 2 lemons and 2 tbsp Limoncello to jelly.*

James says...

I've used a lemon jelly as it does not affect the colour or flavour of any of the variations of soufflé used here.

Index of recipes

continues.